Being a Scientist

Young learners need to know that scientists are not just workers wearing white jackets in laboratories. We do science when we

- cook breakfast
- mix paints to make new colors
- plant seeds in the garden
- watch a squirrel in a tree
- mark how tall we are on a growth chart, or
- look outside to see what the weather is like

The activities in this book relate to the National Science Education Standards (Science as Inquiry). When you follow the step-by-step lessons, your students will be doing science. They will

- observe
- predict
- compare
- order
- categorize

- ask meaningful questions
- conduct investigations
- record information
- communicate investigations and explanations
- use tools and equipment

What makes this book easy for you?

- The step-by-step activities are easy to understand and include illustrations where it's important.
- The resources you need are at your fingertips: record sheets; logbook sheets; and other reproducibles such as minibooks, task cards, and picture cards.
- Each science concept is presented in a self-contained section. You can decide to do the entire book or pick only those sections that enhance your own curriculum.

minibooks

task cards

logbooks

picture cards

Using Logbooks as Learning Tools

ScienceWorks for Kids emphasizes the use of logbooks to help students summarize and solidify learning.

Logbooks are valuable learning tools for several reasons:

• Logbooks give students an opportunity to put what they are learning into their own words.

• Putting ideas into words is an important step in internalizing new information. Whether spoken or written, this experience allows students to synthesize their thinking.

• Explaining and describing experiences helps students make connections between several concepts and ideas.

• Logbook entries allow the teacher to catch misunderstandings right away and then reteach.

• Logbooks are a useful reference for students and a record of what has been learned.

Two Types of Logbooks

This picture stands for class logbook

Throughout the unit, a class logbook will be used to record student understanding.

• Use large sheets of chart paper.

• Hold the pages together with metal rings.

Even though your students may not be reading, the responses can be read to them as a means of confirming and reviewing learning.

This picture stands for student logbook

page 3

Students process their understanding of investigations by writing or drawing their own responses in individual student logbooks. Following the investigations are record and activity sheets that can be added to each student's logbook.

At the conclusion of the unit, reproduce a copy of the logbook cover on page 3 for each student. Students organize their pages and staple them with the cover.

My Logbook

Earth

Name:

My Logbook

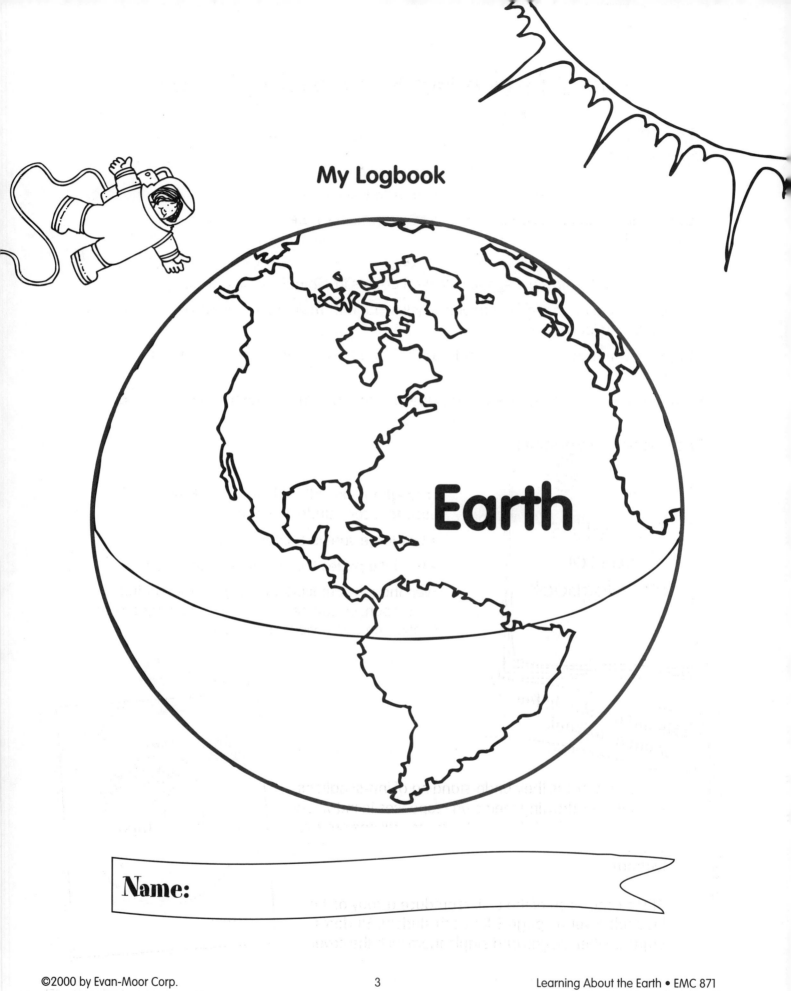

Earth

Name:

Teacher Preparation

Prepare the following before beginning the unit:

• Have a large globe of the earth available. You may be able to borrow a globe of the moon from a high school science teacher.

• Gather rocks of different sizes, colors, textures, and weights. Lapidary shops and landscaping suppliers have a wide variety to choose from.

• Make a class set of "clipboards" for students to use when doing outside observations.

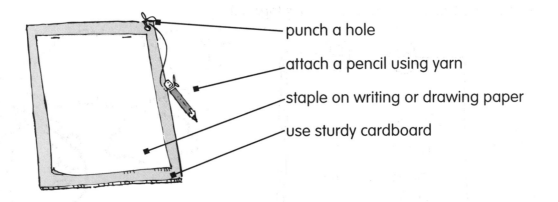

punch a hole

attach a pencil using yarn

staple on writing or drawing paper

use sturdy cardboard

An Earth, Sun, and Moon Library

Gather an assortment of books about the earth, sun, and moon. (See the inside back cover for a bibliography to use throughout the unit.)

Note: *Use the most up-to-date materials you can find to teach the latest scientific discoveries.*

If you include make-believe stories in which inanimate objects talk and display other attributes they don't really have, talk about which actions are true and not true.

Word Usage Note:
Earth is capitalized when it is used as the name of the planet. *(We live on Earth. Mars is the closest planet to Earth.)*

Earth is not capitalized when preceded by *our* or *the*. *(We live on the earth. Mars is the closest planet to our earth.)*

Objects in the sky can be seen and described.

In the Day Sky

- Give each student a clipboard, a sheet of drawing paper, and a crayon. Take your students outside to observe what can be seen in the sky. Have students draw or list what they see. Return to the classroom to share what was seen.

- Create a master list of what was seen on a sheet of chart paper entitled "In the Day Sky." This will become the first page of the class logbook.

In the Day Sky
We saw
birds   sun
airplanes   kite
clouds

- Use student observation notes as the first page of their student logbooks.

- Review the list, asking students to describe the items seen. *(I saw a big black bird. It was flying in the sky. A jet plane flew by. It made noise. There were white clouds in the sky.)* Then have students sort the items into various categories (living/nonliving; far away/nearby; a part of the earth/not a part of the earth).

Help students understand that objects such as birds, airplanes, and clouds are considered "a part of the earth" even though they are in the sky, while the sun in the sky is "not a part of the earth" because it is so far away.

In the Night Sky

- Ask students to think about the kinds of things they see in the sky at night. Give each student a copy of page 9 to take home. They are to look at the night sky and draw what they see, then return the page to school.

  When the forms are returned, repeat the process used for the "In the Day Sky" observation.

  After sharing what students saw in the night sky, place student pages in their individual logbooks.

- Read and discuss the minibook on pages 10 and 11.

page 9

pages 10 and 11

We See the Sun

- Remind students that our sun is a star. Have them describe the sun. (The depth of the description will depend on students' prior knowledge.)

  Use questioning to help students verbalize that the sun is a ball of burning gases that provides us with light and heat.

- Record student responses about the sun on a chart for the class logbook.

- Read and discuss appropriate sections of *The Sun: Our Very Own Star* by Jeanne Bendick and/or *Sun* by Susan Canizares and Daniel Moreton. Make additions or corrections to the chart.

- Using page 12, students write about the sun for their logbooks.

We See the Moon

- Have students describe the moon. Add student responses to the "We see the sun and the moon" chart.

The moon shines at night. It looks big sometimes and little sometimes.

- Read and discuss appropriate parts of *The Moon Book* by Gail Gibbons.

- Using page 13, students write about the moon for their logbooks.

- Explain to students that the moon does not produce light. The following experiment on reflection will help show how we can see the moon.

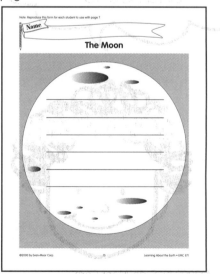

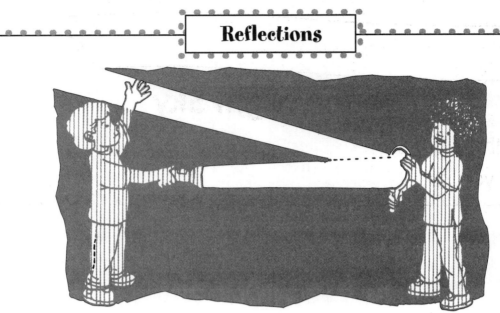

Materials (for each group)
- mirror
- flashlight
- record sheet on page 14, reproduced for each student

Steps to Follow

1. One member of the group holds the flashlight. A second person holds the mirror tilted slightly.

2. Shut the curtains and turn off the lights.

3. The flashlight is pointed at the mirror and turned on. Group members observe closely what happens to the beam of light.

4. Turn the lights back on and ask students to describe what they saw. *(When the flashlight was pointed at the mirror, the light bounced off and we could see other things in the classroom.)*

   Explain that the sun's light shines on the moon just like the flashlight shone on the mirror. The sunlight is reflected away from the moon just as the light was reflected off the mirror. Neither the mirror nor the moon produces light. They both reflect light.

5. Using page 14, students record what they observed by drawing the path of the light beam from the flashlight to the mirror and then the reflected light from the mirror.

- Place completed record sheets in students' logbooks.

- Read *Day Light, Night Light: Where Light Comes From* by Franklyn M. Branley and/or appropriate parts of *The Moon Book*. Make changes or additions to the class logbook.

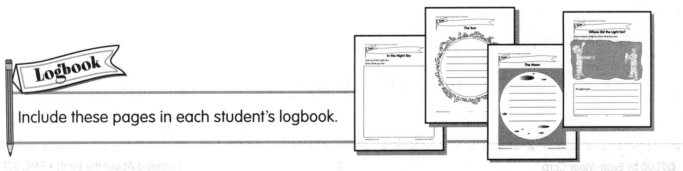

Logbook

Include these pages in each student's logbook.

Name

In the Night Sky

Look up at the night sky.

Draw what you see.

Learning About the Earth • EMC 871

In The Sky

Name:

What do we see in the sky?

birds

kites

clouds

We see the sun in the daytime.

2

moon

We see many stars at night.
We see the moon at night.

stars

Sometimes we see it in the daytime.

3

Earth

Our earth is in the sky, too.

4

Name

The Sun

Name

The Moon

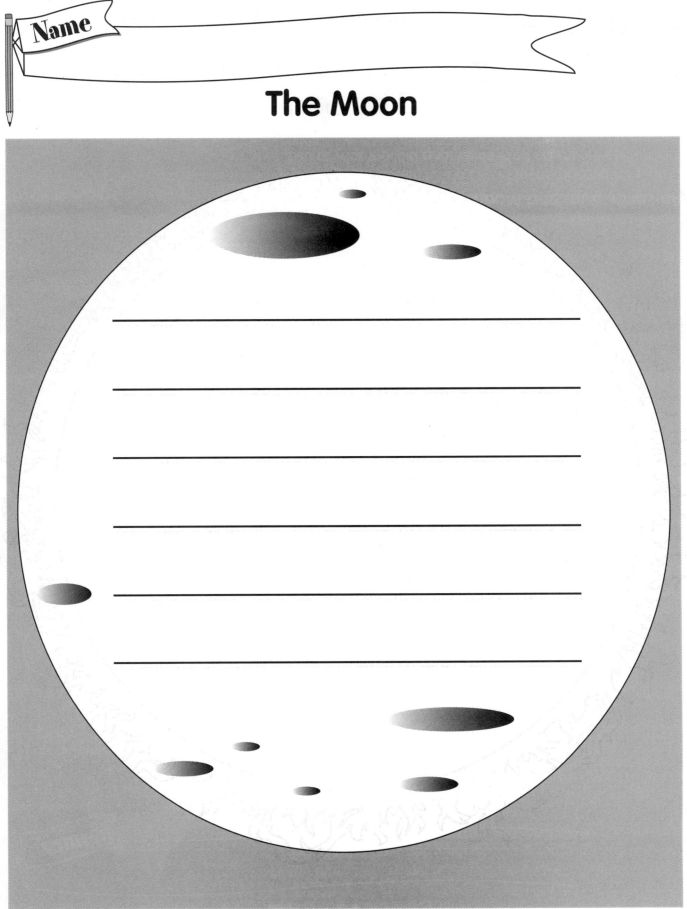

Name

Where Did the Light Go?

Draw a beam of light to show what you saw.

The light beam _____

_____

_____

_____

The sun provides light and heat for Earth.

Why Do We Need the Sun?

- Ask, "Why is the sun important to Earth?" Use guided questions to help students reach these understandings: Plants need light to grow. People and animals need plants for food. Without heat from the sun, Earth would be too cold for people, plants, and animals to live.

- Read and discuss the minibook on pages 16 and 17.

  Ask students to recall what they learned about energy from the sun. Record their comments on a chart.

- Read appropriate parts of *Energy from the Sun* by Allan Fowler and/or *The Sun: Our Very Own Star* by Jeanne Bendick. Make additions to the chart.

- Using page 18, students circle the things that need sunlight (energy from the sun).

Teacher Demonstration–Energy from the Sun

1. Use a candle to model the sun. Close the curtains and turn out the lights. Ask students to tell what they see. Light the candle. Now have them tell what they can see. Have them describe the light source. *(The candle is burning. It makes light.)*

2. Place your hand near enough to the candle to feel the heat. Ask, "What am I feeling when I do this?" *(It is hot.)* Ask students to explain where the heat is coming from. *(It is hot when things burn. The burning candle makes heat.)*

3. Have students explain how the candle acts like the sun. *(The sun is burning and it makes light and heat.)*

   Note: *Remind students not to use candles and matches without adult supervision.*

Include this page in each student's logbook.

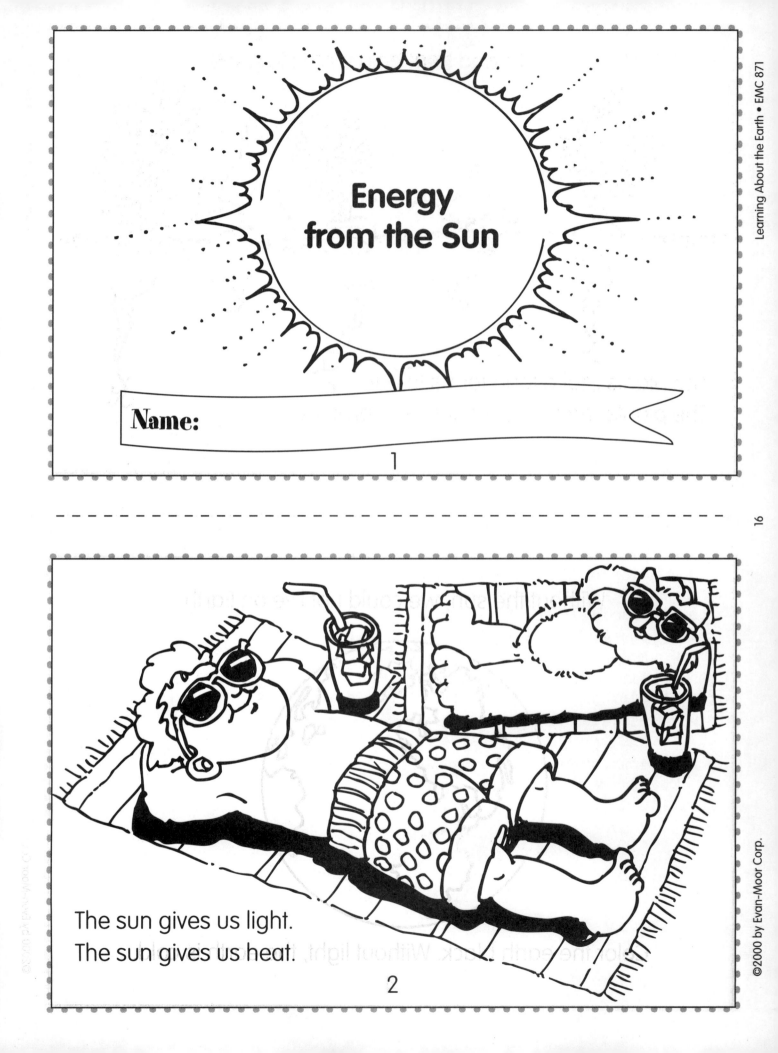

Energy from the Sun

Name:

1

The sun gives us light.
The sun gives us heat.

2

Learning About the Earth • EMC 871

Sunlight and heat help plants to grow.

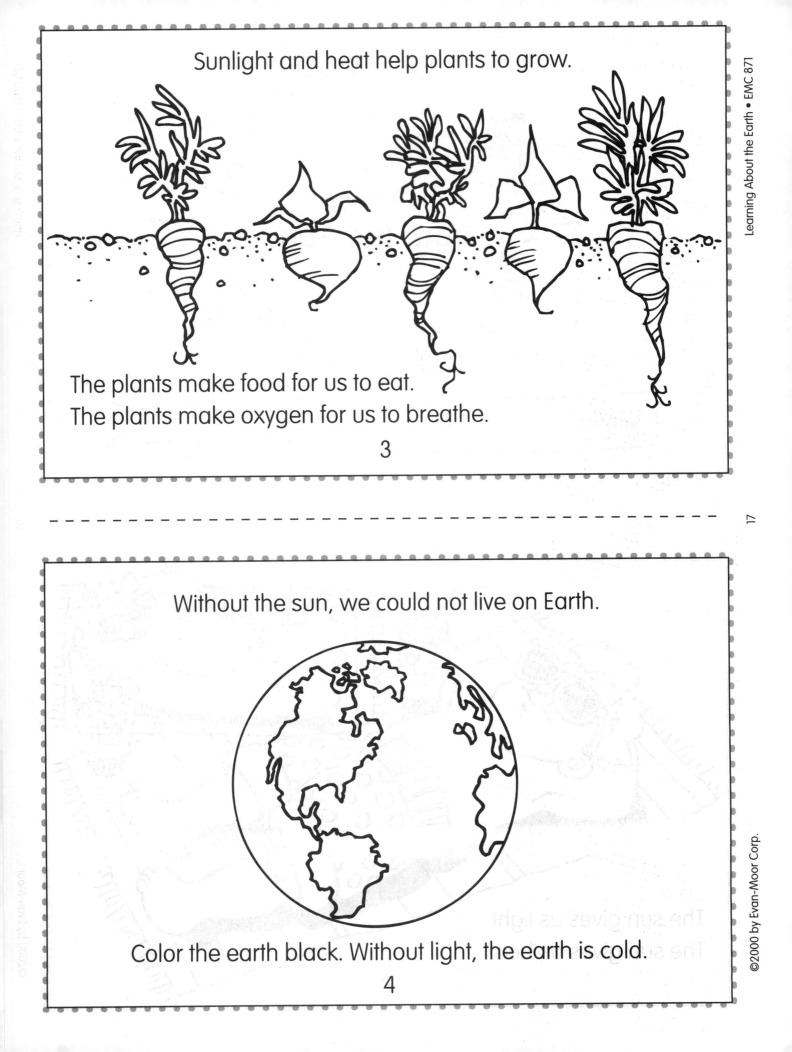

The plants make food for us to eat.
The plants make oxygen for us to breathe.

3

Learning About the Earth • EMC 871

Without the sun, we could not live on Earth.

Color the earth black. Without light, the earth is cold.

4

Name

We Need the Sun

Circle the things that need sunlight.

Objects in the sky have patterns of movement.

Day and Night

- Say, "One of the things you saw in the sky during the day was the sun. Do you see the sun in the sky at night? Can you think of a reason why you can't see the sun?"

- Read and discuss *The Sun Is Always Shining Somewhere* by Allan Fowler or appropriate parts of *Sun Up, Sun Down* by Gail Gibbons.

Note: *Understanding that the earth, not the sun, is moving isn't easy for young students. Do this demonstration only if your students are ready.*

As the Earth Turns—A Demonstration

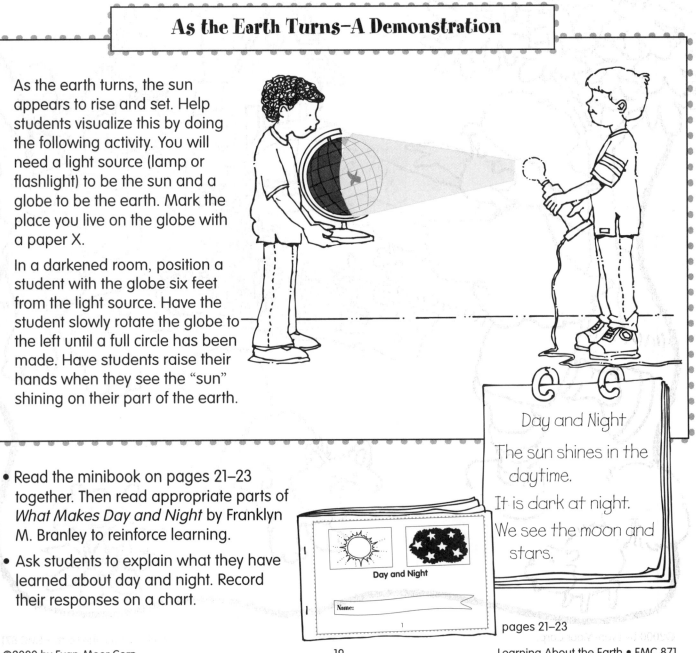

As the earth turns, the sun appears to rise and set. Help students visualize this by doing the following activity. You will need a light source (lamp or flashlight) to be the sun and a globe to be the earth. Mark the place you live on the globe with a paper X.

In a darkened room, position a student with the globe six feet from the light source. Have the student slowly rotate the globe to the left until a full circle has been made. Have students raise their hands when they see the "sun" shining on their part of the earth.

Day and Night

The sun shines in the daytime.

It is dark at night.

We see the moon and stars.

Day and Night

Name:

1

pages 21–23

- Read the minibook on pages 21–23 together. Then read appropriate parts of *What Makes Day and Night* by Franklyn M. Branley to reinforce learning.

- Ask students to explain what they have learned about day and night. Record their responses on a chart.

The Moon Changes

- Ask students to recall what they know about the moon. Explain that the moon looks a little different each day. (Some events in nature have a repeating pattern.) Ask students to describe the changes they've noticed.

- Read *I'll See You When the Moon Is Full* by Susi Gregg Fowler to introduce the phases of the moon.

- Review what students have learned about the moon. Write the information on a chart.

- Make a large "Moon Calendar" on a bulletin board in the classroom. Assign one student per night the task of looking at the moon and drawing what is seen (see the form on page 24). Attach the returned forms in order on the bulletin board for a complete cycle of changes.

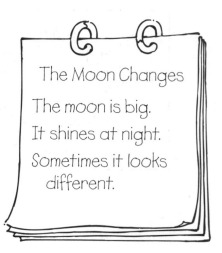

The Moon Changes

The moon is big.

It shines at night.

Sometimes it looks different.

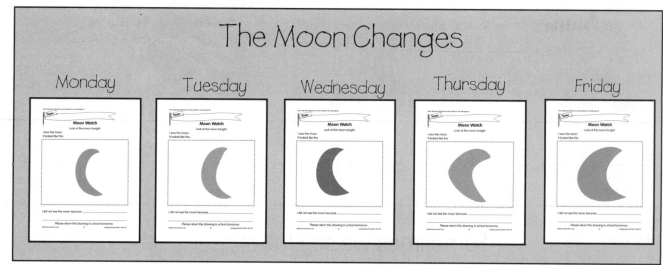

- Read and discuss *So That's How the Moon Changes Shape!* by Allan Fowler or appropriate parts of *The Moon Book* by Gail Gibbons. Make additions and changes to the chart.

Then make the "Phases of the Moon" wheel on page 25. Review the phases of the moon with students before they take the wheels home to share with parents.

Note: *Turn the wheel clockwise for phases to appear in the correct order.*

page 25

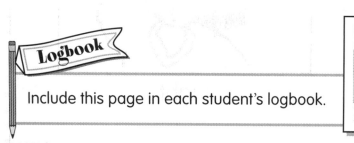

Include this page in each student's logbook.

Learning About the Earth • EMC 871

Day and Night

Name:

1

Sometimes we see the sun.
Sometimes we don't.

day

night

2

The sun shines, making light.

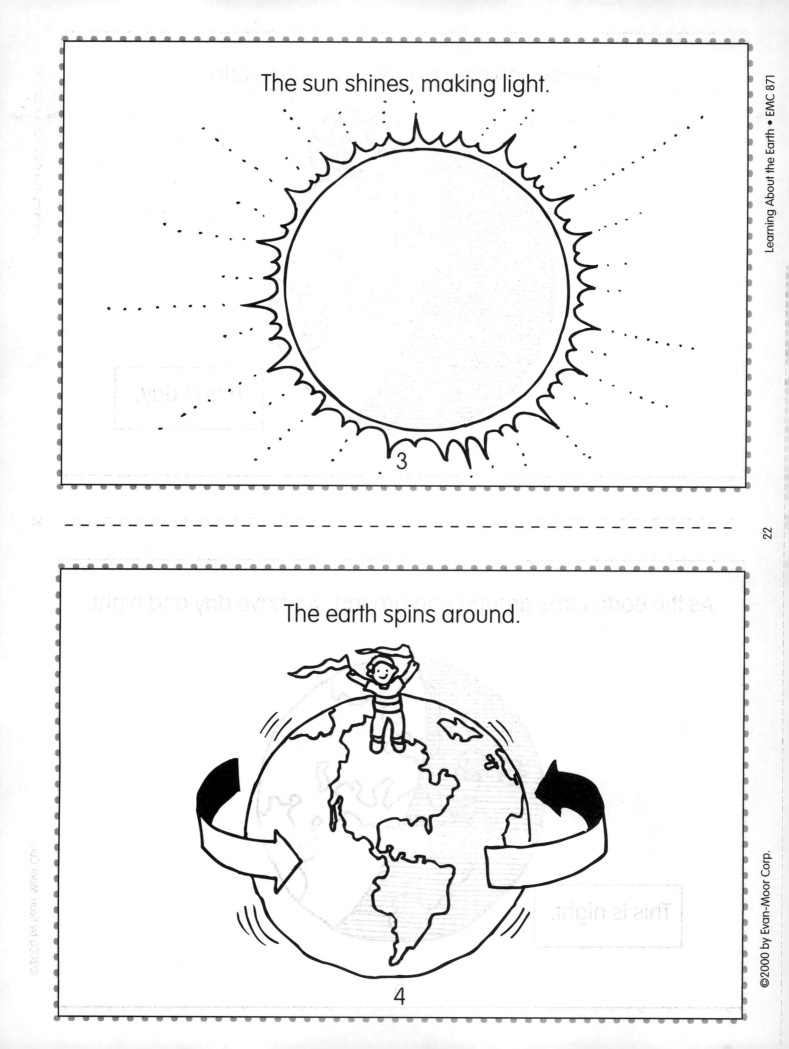

3

The earth spins around.

4

The sun shines on one side of the earth.

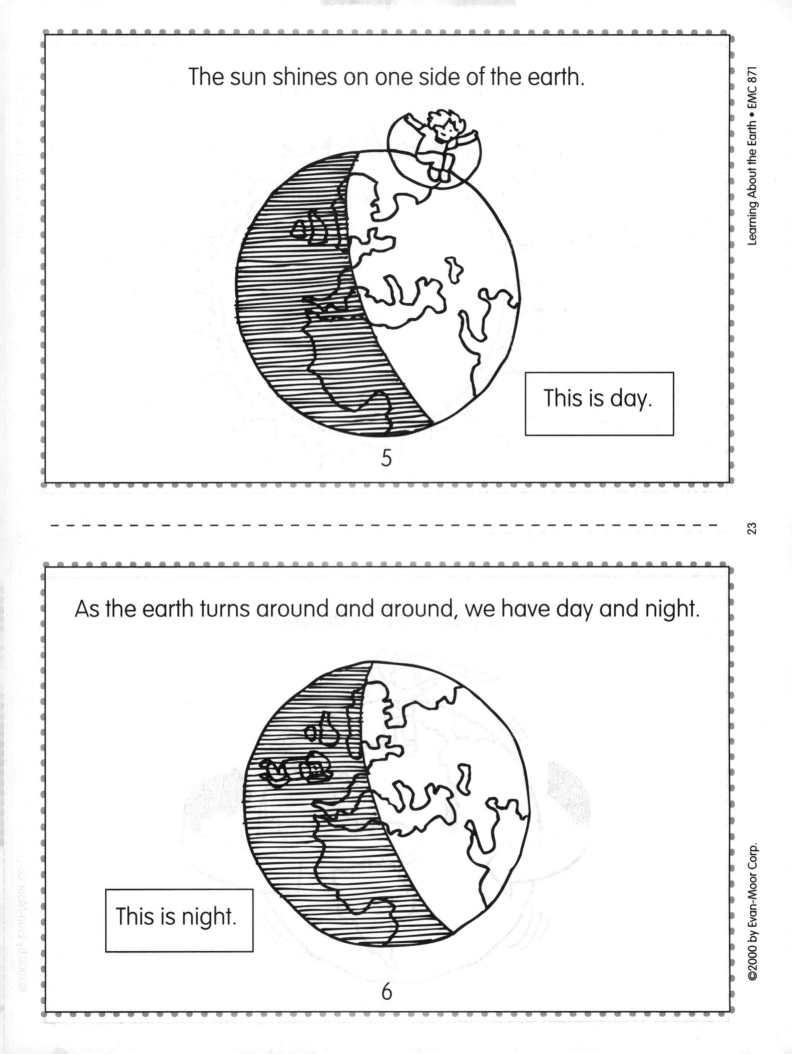

This is day.

5

Learning About the Earth • EMC 871

As the earth turns around and around, we have day and night.

This is night.

6

Name

Moon Watch

Look at the moon tonight.

I saw the moon.
It looked like this.

I did not see the moon because _____

_____ .

Please return this drawing to school tomorrow.

          Learning About the Earth • EMC 871

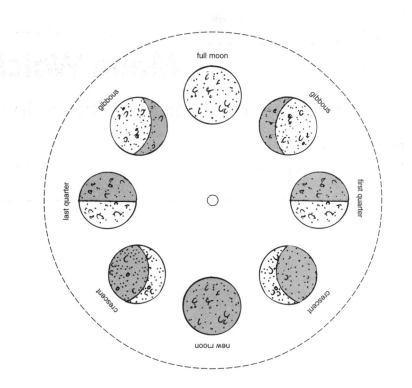

1. Color.
2. Cut it out.
3. Fasten the wheel
   inside the folder.

The earth is surrounded by air.

Air Is Everywhere

- Remove the lid of an empty box and show students the inside. Ask them to describe it. *(It's empty.)* Explain that the box is really full of something. Ask students what is in it. Take suggestions. If the students don't guess the correct answer, tell them that the box is full of air. Explain that there is a blanket of air around the earth. This is the air we breathe.

- Do the following demonstration to prove that air is present even when we can't see or smell it.

Air–A Demonstration

Materials
- large glass bowl of water
- paper towel
- clear plastic drinking glass

Steps to Follow

1. Crumple a paper towel and push it into the bottom of the glass.

2. Keep the glass upside down and push it underwater.

3. Lift the glass out of the water, keeping it straight up and down.

4. Turn it right side up and take out the paper towel. Ask, "What happened?" *(The towel is dry.)* "Why didn't the water touch the paper towel? *(There was air in the glass. It kept the water from touching the towel.)*

5. Repeat the demonstration, this time tilting the glass to let the air escape. Draw students' attention to the bubbles that rise in the bowl. Ask, "What are those bubbles?" Remove the paper towel and have students describe it. *(It is wet.)* Ask them to explain why the towel got wet this time. *(There wasn't any air to keep the water away from the towel.)*

6. Using page 28, students draw pictures to show what happened.

page 28

Note: Reproduce this form for each student to use with page 26.

Name

Air Is Everywhere

Match.

- Place the investigation materials at a classroom science center so students can explore on their own.

- Read the minibook on page 29 and appropriate parts of *Air is All Around You* by Franklyn M. Branley and *If We Could See the Air* by David Suzuki. Discuss some of the ways that we know air is all around us.

- Record student responses about air for the class logbook.

page 29

Making Connections

- Have students draw three things in the classroom that are filled with air. As students report back to the class, ask them to explain how they know that there is air in the objects they drew.

- Have students bring an object from home that contains air. Again, have students explain how they know the object contains air.

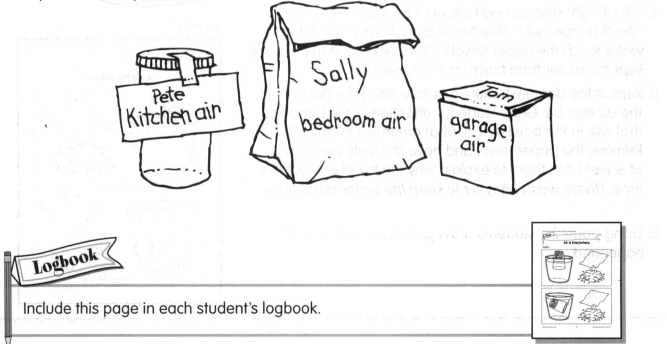

Logbook

Include this page in each student's logbook.

Air Is Everywhere

Match.

1

The earth is covered by a
blanket of air.

Air Is All Around

4

But we can feel it
when it is moving.

The air is all around us.

2

We can't see it.
We can't smell it.

3

fold 1

fold 2

The Earth Is a Sphere

- Brainstorm to create a list of things that are round like a ball. Write all answers on the chalkboard. Introduce the term *sphere*. Use real objects to clarify the difference between a circle and a sphere (plate, ball, globe, penny, etc.). Hold up an object and ask, "Is this a circle or a sphere?" Next, go through the list on the chalkboard to determine which items are spheres and which are circles.

- Using page 33, students identify the spheres.

page 33

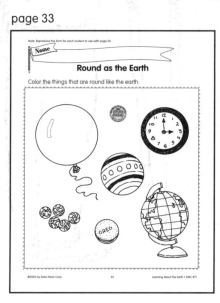

Round or Flat?

- Take your students outside to look at the horizon line. Ask them to tell you what shape the earth appears to be. Explain that although the earth looks flat, it is really a sphere.

  Show students a globe and a map. Explain that they both represent the earth. Ask students to tell which one looks more like the real earth and why. Name other spheres in the sky that have been learned about (sun, moon).

- Using page 34, students complete the sentences and color the picture that shows the shape of the entire earth.

page 34

Learning About the Earth • EMC 871

Covering the Earth

- Have students name items that cover the earth. Begin with things they can see where they live *(soil, plants, lake, hills, etc.)*. Then ask them to think of other things they have seen *(mountains, ocean, rivers, forests, etc.)*.

  Show the pictures of the water and landforms on pages 35–38 to stimulate more answers. List the items named on the chalkboard.

- Go back through the list to sort the items. Circle landforms and underline water forms.

- Write a description of the earth and its water and landforms.

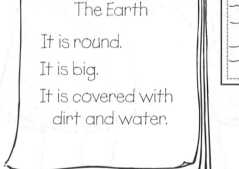

pages 35–38

- Read and discuss *The Earth Is Mostly Ocean* by Allan Fowler and appropriate parts of *Our Earth* by Anne F. Rockwell.

- Using page 39, students draw a waterscape and a landscape.

- Students follow the directions in "Paint the Earth" on page 32 to create pictures of the earth, showing land and water.

page 39

Paint the Earth

Materials

- fingerpaint paper cut into plate-sized circles
- fingerpaint—blue, green, brown
- newspapers and paper towels
- paint smocks

Preparation

Cover work areas with newspaper. Have students wear smocks, with their sleeves rolled up. Have two paper towels available for each student. (One to wipe the dripping paint off and one to hold in the paint hand as they walk to the clean-up area. This will minimize the temptation to touch someone with a paint-covered hand.)

Steps to Follow

1. Pass out the paper circles.

2. Put a puddle of blue fingerpaint (or mix liquid starch and tempera paint) in the center of the circle. Students cover the paper circle with the blue paint.

3. Drop a bit of green and/or brown paint in the center of the blue circle. Students move this paint around to create "land" on their planet.

4. Allow the paint to dry thoroughly before moving the artwork.

5. While the paint is drying, help students write a sentence or two describing the earth. Paste the sentences to the backs of their paintings. Take the paintings home to share.

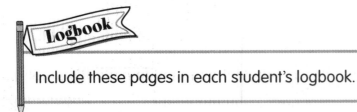

Logbook

Include these pages in each student's logbook.

Name

Round as the Earth

Color the things that are round like the earth.

Note: Reproduce this form for each student to use with page 30.

Name

Round or Flat?

From the sky, the earth looks _____ .

From the land, the earth looks _____ .

34

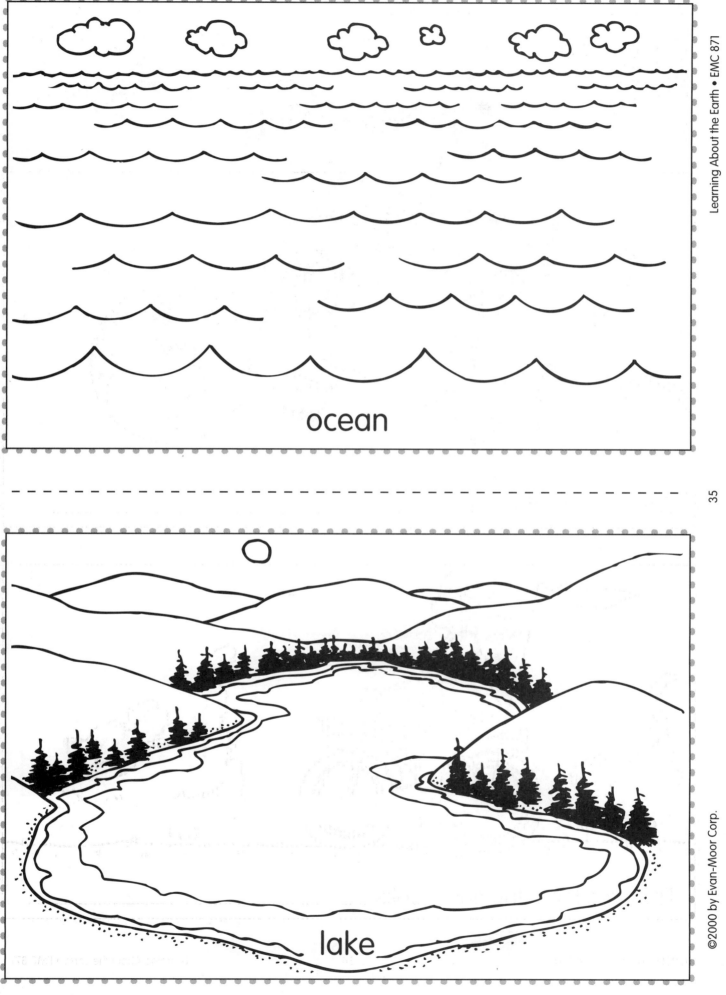

ocean

lake

Learning About the Earth • EMC 871

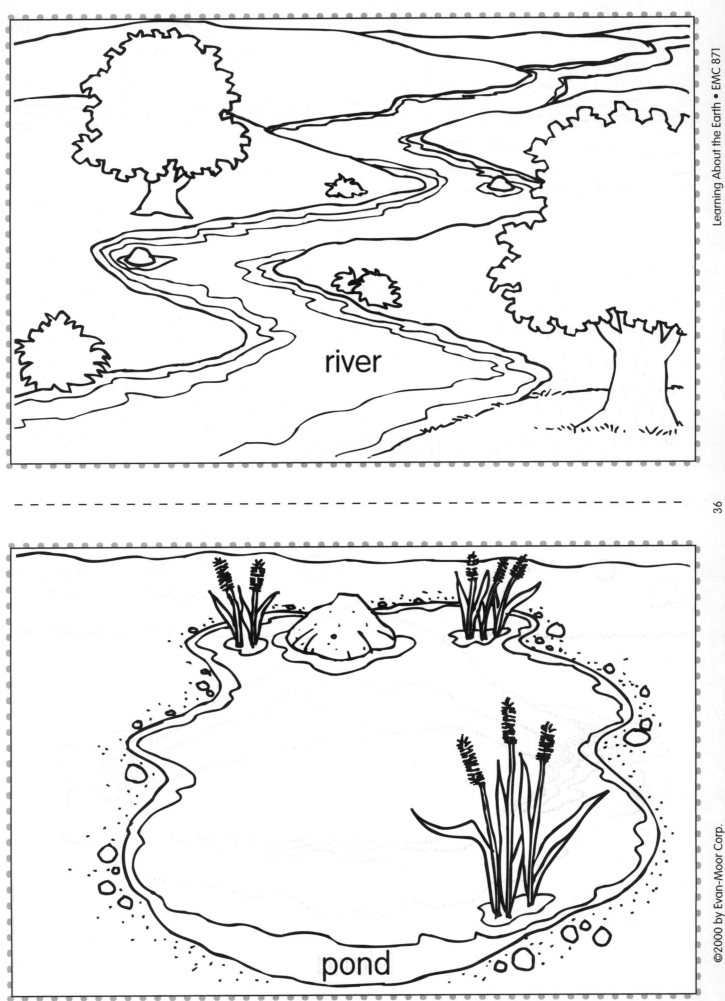

river

pond

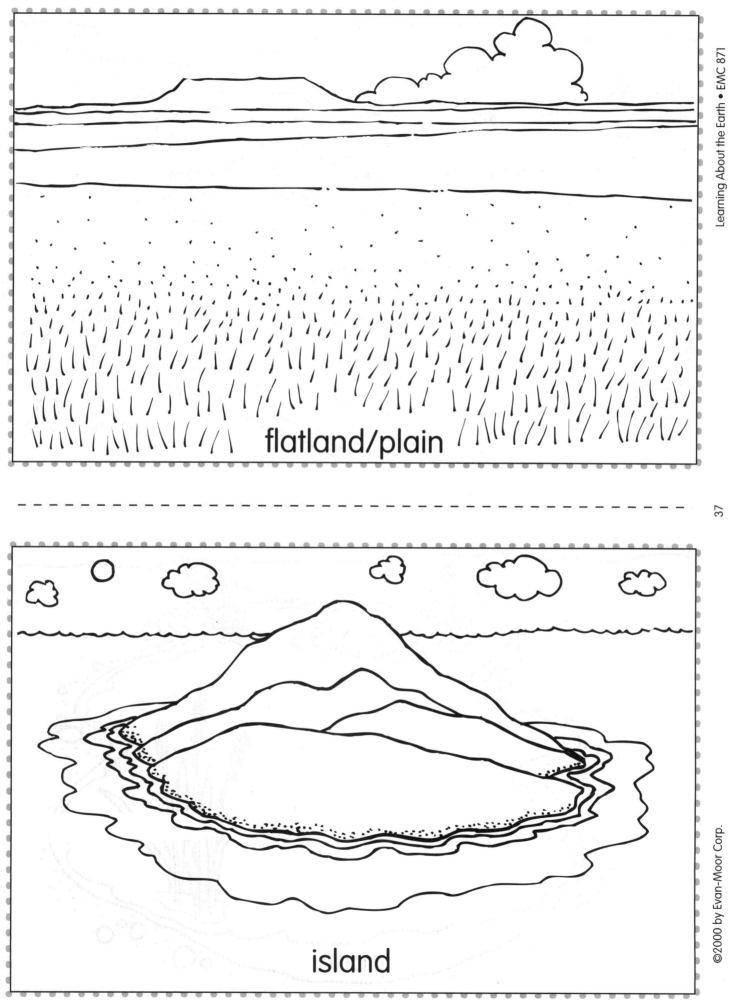

flatland/plain

island

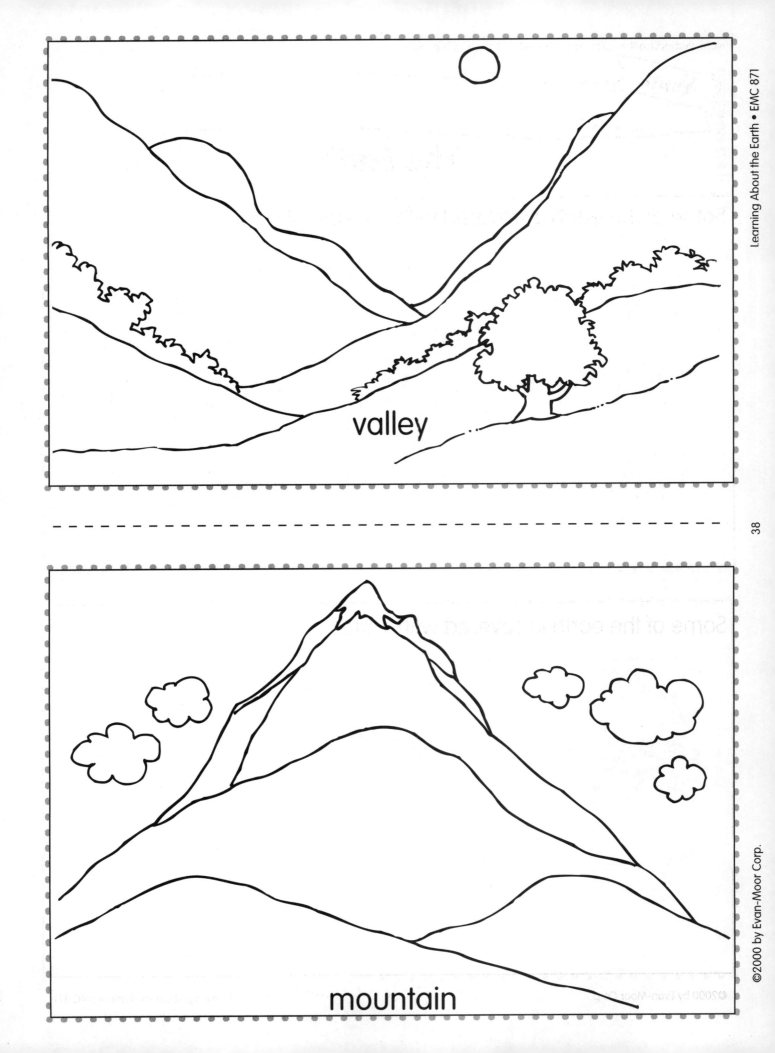

valley

mountain

Name

The Earth

Some of the earth is covered with soil and plants.

Some of the earth is covered with water.

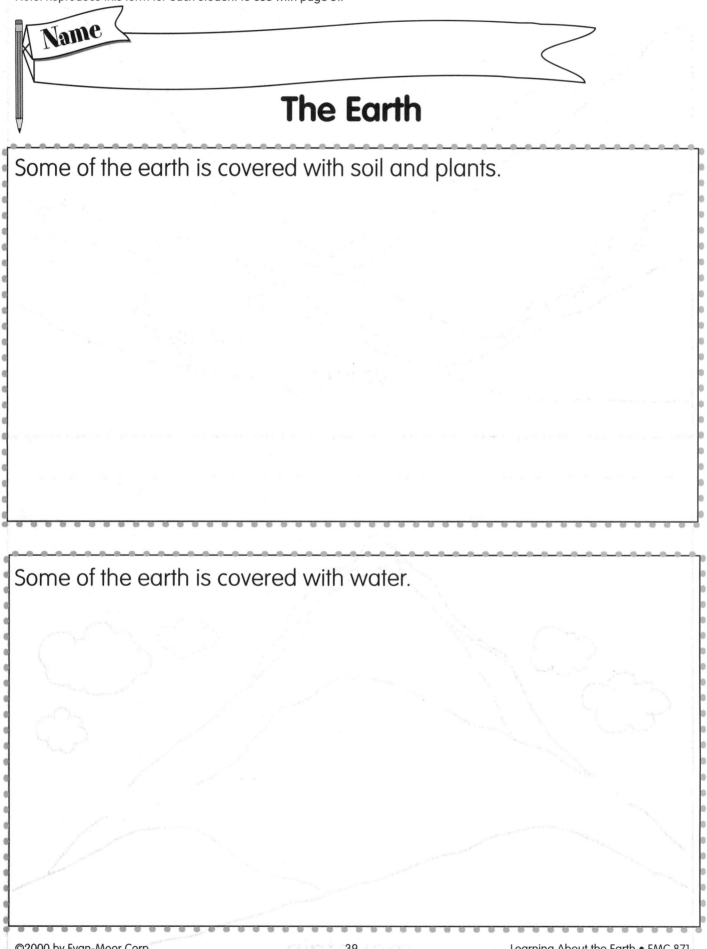

The earth is a sphere of rock.

The Earth Is a Sphere of Rock

- Show students an unsliced loaf of bread. Ask, "What is the outside part of this bread called?" *(It's the crust.)* Cut off a slice of bread to show how different it looks under the crust.

crust

- Explain that the earth has a crust, too. But most of the earth's crust is covered by plants, soil, or water. Under the crust of the earth is rock. Use illustrations from books such as *They Could Still be Mountains* or *It Could Still Be a Rock*, both by Allan Fowler, to illustrate the rock that is found under the crust.

- Read and discuss the minibook on pages 41–43 and appropriate parts of *It Could Still Be a Rock*. Add to the description of the earth begun on page 31.

The Earth

It is round. It is big.
It is covered with dirt and water.

It has a crust. The crust is covered with dirt and water.

Rock Is Everywhere

Name:

1

crust

pages 41–43

Rock Collections

You will need a great variety of rocks to use in the upcoming rock investigations. Take students on a walk or field trip to collect rocks. Purchase interesting rocks from lapidary shops and landscaping or building supply centers, and have students bring rocks from home. Use the rocks to create two types of rock collections in the classroom.

Class Collection—This is a large supply of rocks that all students can use. This is where really big rocks and any "one-of-a-kind" rocks are kept.

Student Collections—Have each student label an egg carton with his or her name. Put one rock in each cup of the carton. This collection becomes the student's source of rocks for the activities in the next concept.

Rock Is Everywhere

Name:

1

Rock is everywhere
under our feet.

2

Sometimes the rock is covered with soil.

3

Sometimes the rock is covered with water.

4

Under the soil and under the water there is rock!

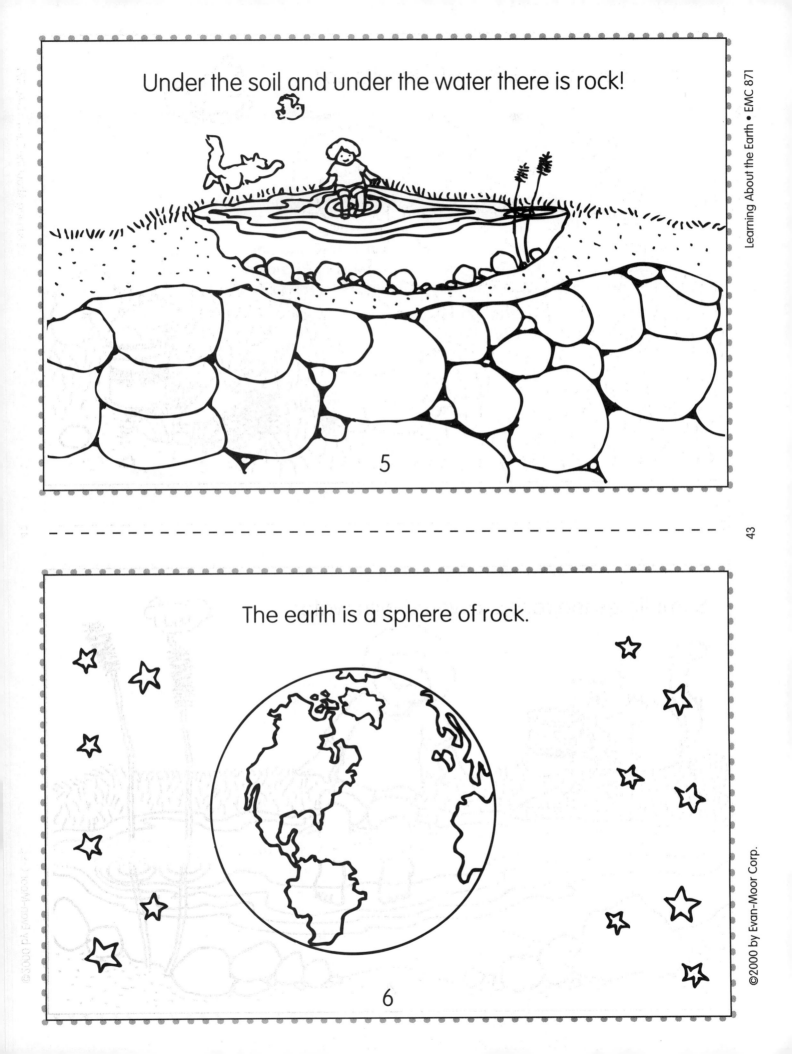

5

The earth is a sphere of rock.

6

Rocks can be described by their physical properties.

Describing Rocks

- Ask students to share what they know about rocks. *(Rocks are hard. Some rocks are smooth. A lot of rocks are gray.)*

- Use illustrations of rocks from *Let's Go Rock Collecting* by Roma Gans as you discuss the physical appearance of rocks. Ask, "What are some of the ways rocks are different? Have you ever found a rock that was a pretty color? How many different colors can rocks be?"

- Divide your students into pairs or small groups. Give each group several rocks from the class collection and a hand lens. Allow time for them to look at their rocks carefully, discussing what they see with group members.

- Then, using page 49, have students draw and describe their favorite rock from the collection. Place the completed drawings in students' logbooks.

- Ask students to recall what they have learned about rocks. Record their responses.

Rocks

Rocks are hard.

Rocks are different colors.

Some rocks are big.

page 49

My Favorite Rock

Draw a picture of your rock here.

Tell what your rock looks like.

Learning for Myself

Have students do the experiments on pages 45–47 to explore some of the attributes of rocks.

Rocks Are Many Different Colors

Materials (for each group)

- plastic bowls
- student rock collections
- crayons (include gray)
- water
- hand lens
- paper towels
- record sheet on page 50, reproduced for each student

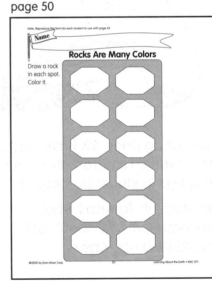

page 50

Steps to Follow

1. Students look at the colors of the rocks in their collections. Then they put their rocks, one at a time, in the dish of water to see if any change occurs. Use the hand lens for an up-close examination. Dry each rock before putting it back into the egg carton.

2. Students draw each rock in one section of the record sheet and then color it to show its color when wet.

3. Have students share the results. Ask, "What happened when you put your rocks in the water? Can you see the color better on a wet rock or a dry one? How many different colors did you have? What color are most of your rocks?"

Place completed record sheets in students' logbooks.

45

Materials (for each group)

- student rock collections
- 2 paper plates—labeled "rough" and "smooth"
- record sheet on page 51, reproduced for each student

Steps to Follow

1. Students feel each of their rocks. They place the rocks with a rough texture on one plate and the rocks with a smooth texture on the other.

2. Share the results. Ask, "Could you tell if a rock was rough or smooth by just looking at it? How many smooth rocks did you have? How many rough rocks did you have? What made some of the rocks feel rough?"

3. Students complete their record sheets.

   Note: *You may want to point out that some rocks seem to be made up of many types of materials and other rocks seem to be made up of only one type of material. Have students use hand lenses to examine the rocks closely.*

   Place completed record sheets in students' logbooks.

page 51

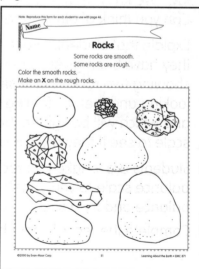

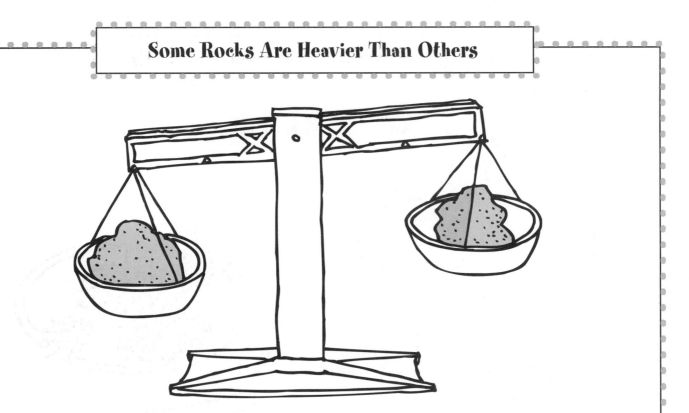

Materials (for each group)
- balance scale
- rocks of assorted sizes and weights (include pumice or other very light rocks in the assortment)
- record sheet on page 52, reproduced for each student

page 52

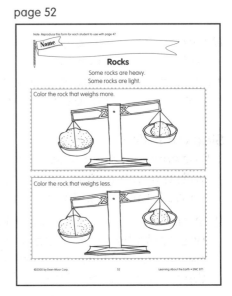

Steps to Follow

1. Say, "We know that rocks are different colors and textures. Can you think of other ways they may be different?"

   Explain that students are to find out which of the rocks they have been given is the heaviest. Model the task by showing two rocks. Have students try to tell, first by looking and then by feeling, which rock will be heavier and which will be lighter. Weigh the rocks on a balance scale to see if they are correct.

2. Students are to take two rocks at a time, estimate which will be heavier, and then use the balance scale to verify their prediction. Each time, students leave the heavier rock on the balance and try a second rock to see which is heavier, until all rocks have been weighed.

3. Complete the record sheet by circling the correct rock in each box.

4. Share the results.

   Have students share their heaviest rock. Ask, "Was it the rock you thought would be the heaviest? Was your biggest rock the heaviest?"

   Place completed record sheets in students' logbooks.

What Is Sand?

- Give each child a small pile of sand and a hand lens. Have students look at the sand samples closely. Ask students, "What is sand? Where does it come from?" Guide them to discover that sand is small bits of rock. See if they can figure out that sand comes from larger rocks that have been broken into small pieces.

- Ask students to tell you what they learned about sand. *(Sand is made up of little pieces of rock that have broken off big rocks.)* Ask students to think of what might cause big rocks to break up into small bits of sand *(wind, water)*.

- Record student responses on a chart entitled "Sand," and then have them do the following activity to make sand. (This activity requires adult supervision.)

Sand

Sand is little pieces of rock.

Making Sand

Materials
- soft, easily broken rock such as sandstone or talc
- hard stone
- hand lens
- safety goggles
- paper plate

Steps to Follow

1. Students put on safety goggles and then bang the lightweight rock against the hard rock to break off pieces. Continue pounding until very small pieces are created.

2. Pick up the little pieces and put them on the paper plate. Look at the pieces with a hand lens.

3. Allow time for students to share what they learned with classmates. Ask, "How has the rock changed? How are the pieces like the sand you examined earlier? How are they different?" Add any new information to the "Sand" chart.

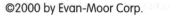 **Logbook**

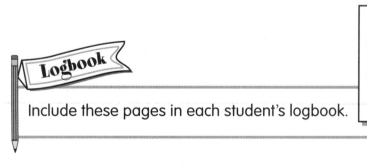

Include these pages in each student's logbook.

                   Learning About the Earth • EMC 871

Name

My Favorite Rock

Draw a picture of your rock here.

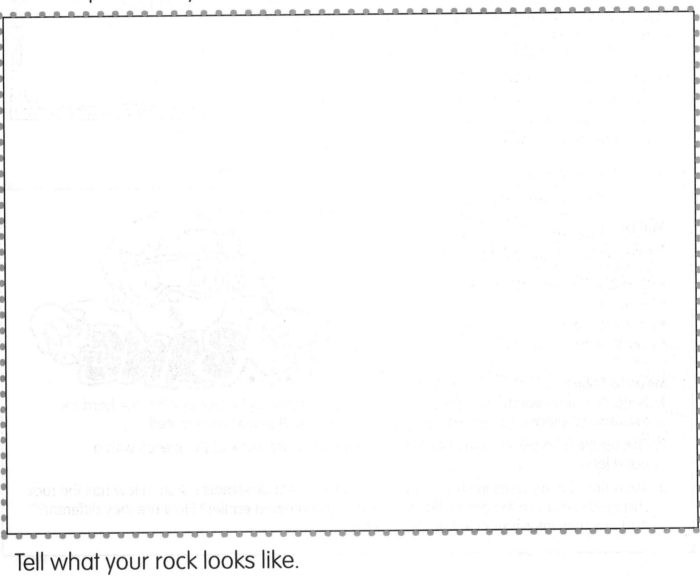

Tell what your rock looks like.

_____

_____

Note: Reproduce this form for each student to use with page 45.

Name

Rocks Are Many Colors

Draw a rock
in each spot.
Color it.

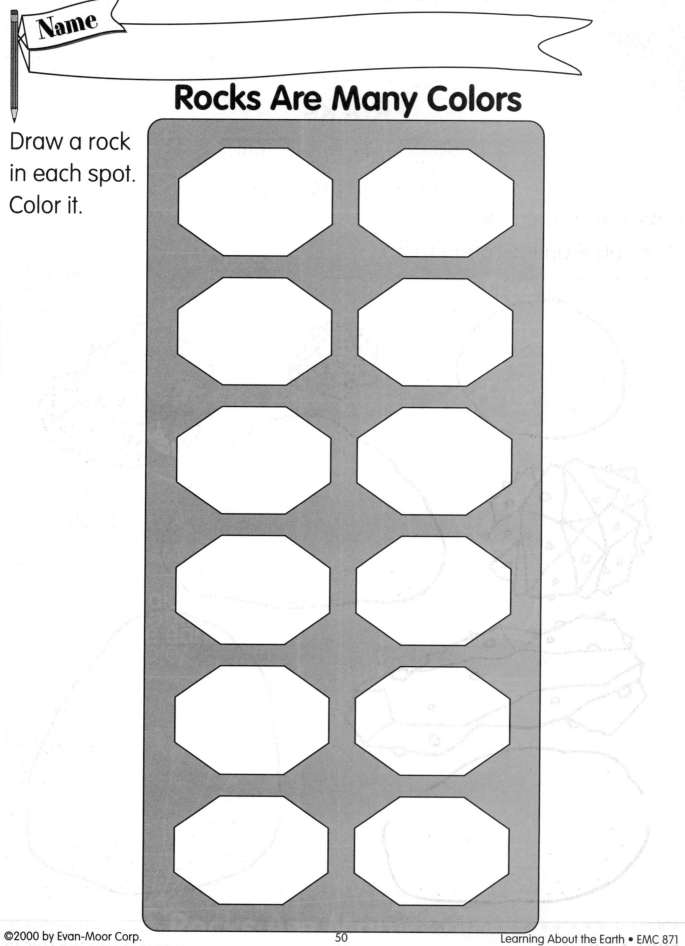

Name

Rocks

Some rocks are smooth.

Some rocks are rough.

Color the smooth rocks.

Make an **X** on the rough rocks.

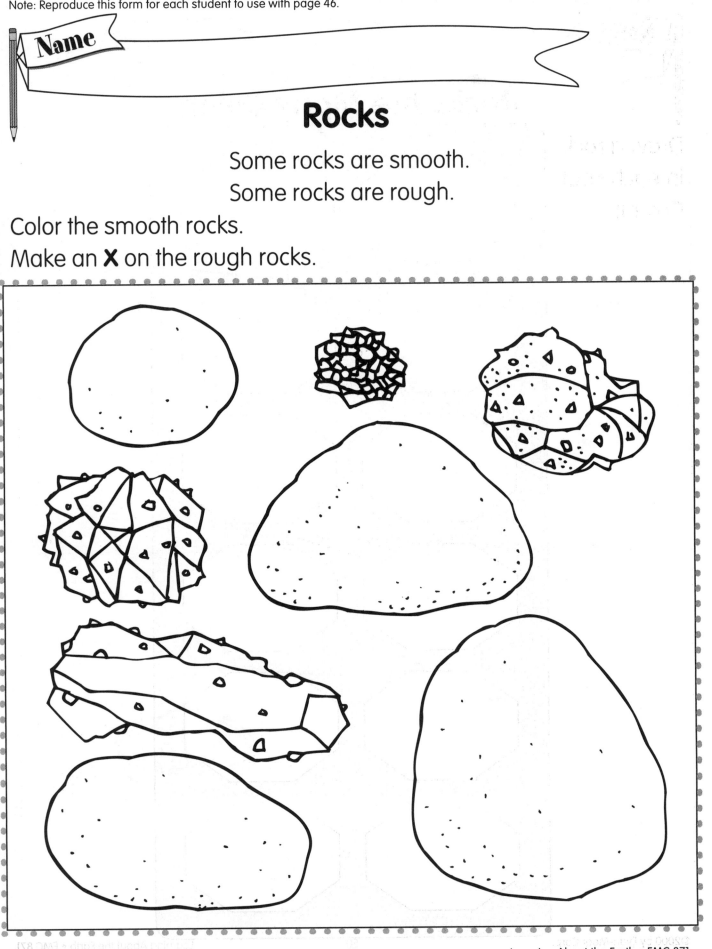

Rocks

Some rocks are heavy.
Some rocks are light.

Color the rock that weighs more.

Color the rock that weighs less.

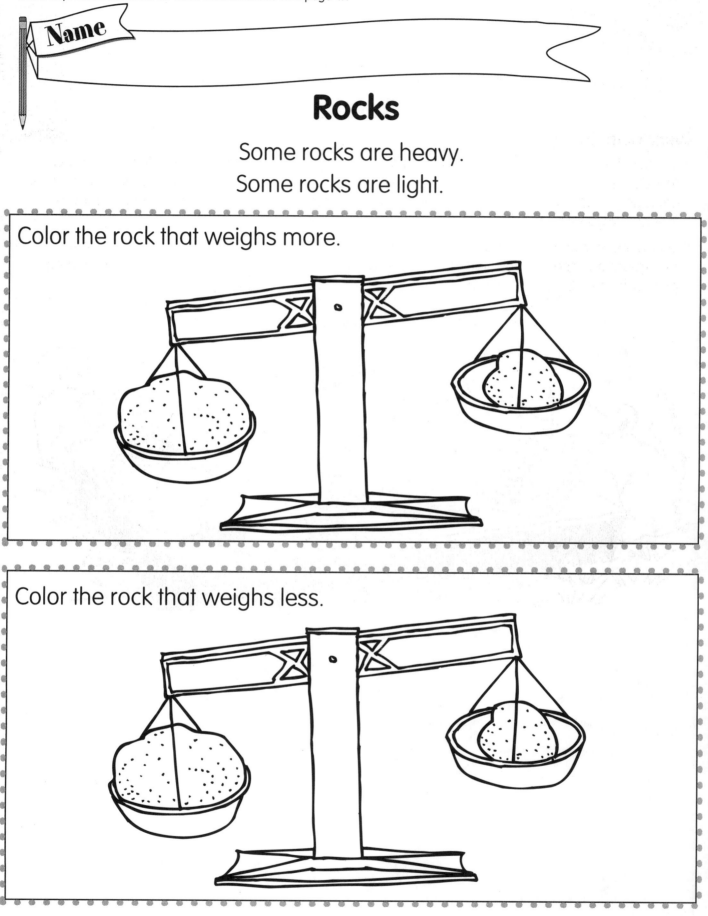

The surface of the earth changes.

Everything Changes

- Discuss the ways your students are changing (getting taller, weighing more, etc.) to introduce the idea that everything changes, even the earth. Explain that the surface of the earth is always changing, too, but it usually takes a very long time. Tell students that they will do experiments to learn ways this happens.

- Do the experiments on page 54 to explore the changes created by wind and water. Use the classroom sandbox. (If you do not have a sandbox in class, make one using a plastic wading pool or large tub filled with sand.)

Wind and water make changes in the sand.

Wind and Water Change the Earth

Materials
- sandbox
- electric fan (adult use only)
- water
- hose or watering can
- overhead transparencies of pages 56 and 58
- record sheets on pages 57, 59, and 60, reproduced for each student

Steps to Follow—Wind

1. Students create sand hills in the sandbox. Ask them to predict what will happen if the wind blows across the hills.

2. Have students stand well back from the sandbox. (You may want to tape off a "child-free" zone around the sandbox.) Place a fan next to the sandbox (pointing in a direction where no students are standing) and turn it on to create a "wind" blowing across the "land."

3. Ask students to describe what happens. Explain that the same thing happens across the land, especially when strong winds are blowing. Use the transparency of page 56 to review how wind changes the surface of the earth.

4. Using page 57, students number the pictures in order.

Steps to Follow—Water

1. Students create sand hills in the sandbox. Ask them to predict what will happen if water flows down the hills. Write their predictions on the chalkboard.

2. Use a hose or large watering can to create a steady stream of water flowing down the hills. (This experiment will work best if you can tilt the sandbox somewhat so the water can run downhill.)

3. Ask students to describe what has happened to the sand. Explain that over time, moving water can make great changes in the surface of landforms.

   Use the transparency of page 58 to review how water changes the surface of the earth.

4. Using page 59, students number the pictures in order.

5. Summarize the two experiments, using page 60.

pages 56 and 58

pages 57, 59, and 60

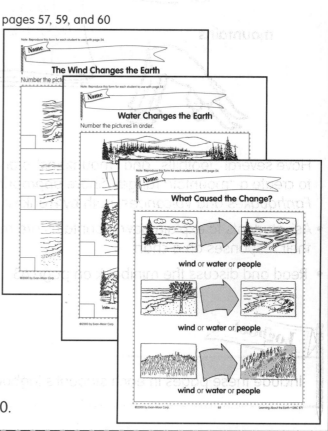

Mountains Change

- Ask students, "What are mountains?" Share pictures of various kinds of mountains (sharp peaks, tall, round, and smooth). *They Could Still Be Mountains* by Allan Fowler contains pictures of various types of mountains.

- Explain that mountains are rock formations that have been pushed up by earthquakes or built by volcanoes. Use overhead transparencies of pages 61 and 62 to help make this clearer. (This is a difficult concept for young children to understand. You may want to leave it at "Mountains are made of rock.")

- Act out the development of a mountain. Students lie on the floor. They arch their backs to become "foothills." Then they rise up on their hands and feet to become "mountains."

pages 61 and 62

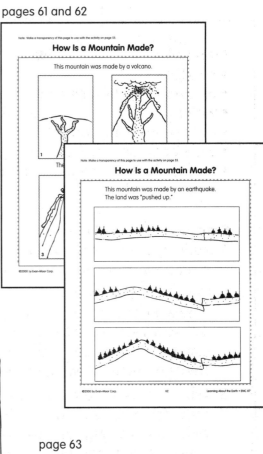

flat

foothills

mountains

Mountains

Mountains are big. They are made of rock. Sometimes land is pushed up to make mountains.

page 63

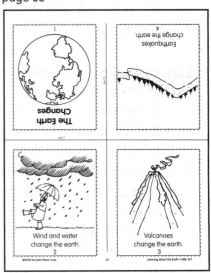

Have several "foothills" and "mountains" stand in a row to create a "mountain range." Share appropriate parts of *Earthquakes* and *Volcanoes*, both by Franklyn M. Branley.

- Ask students to explain how mountains are made. Record their responses on a chart.

- Read and discuss the minibook on page 63.

Logbook

Include these pages in each student's logbook.

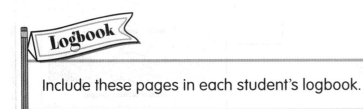

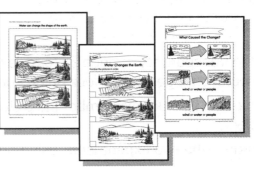

Wind can change the shape of the earth.

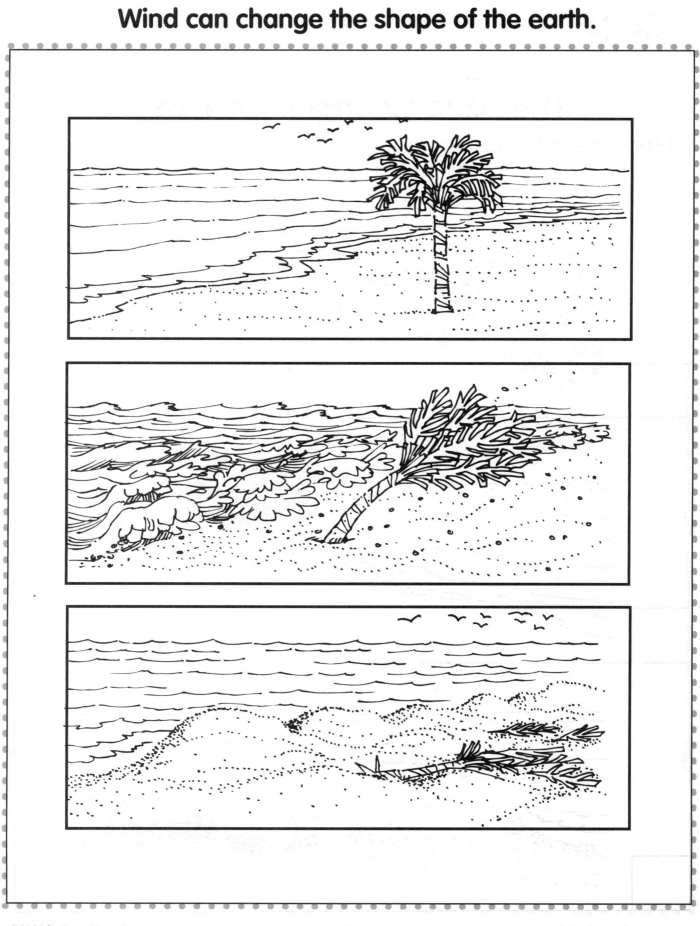

Learning About the Earth • EMC 871

Name

The Wind Changes the Earth

Number the pictures in order.

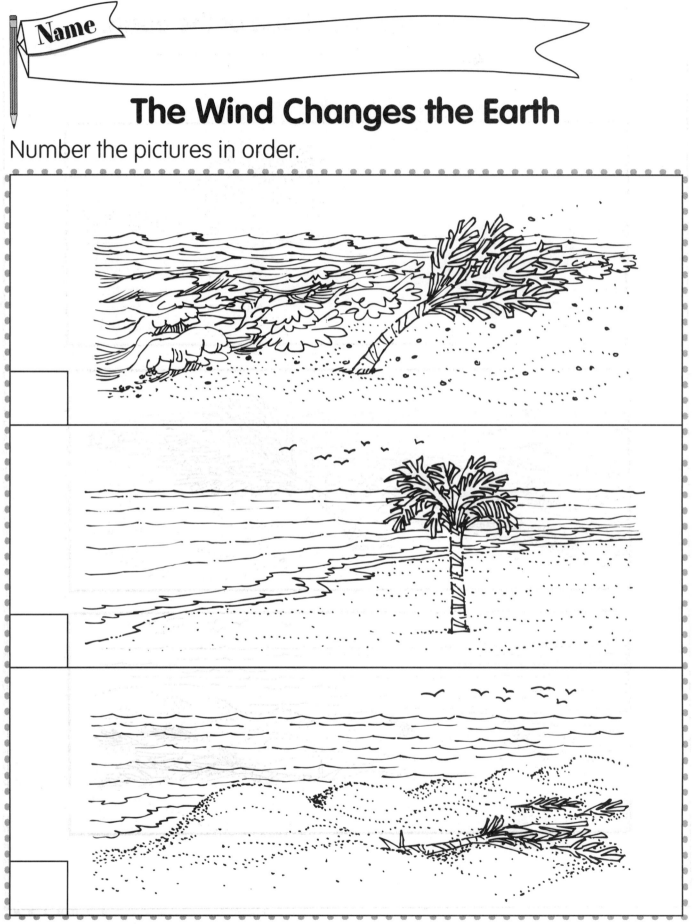

Water can change the shape of the earth.

Name

Water Changes the Earth

Number the pictures in order.

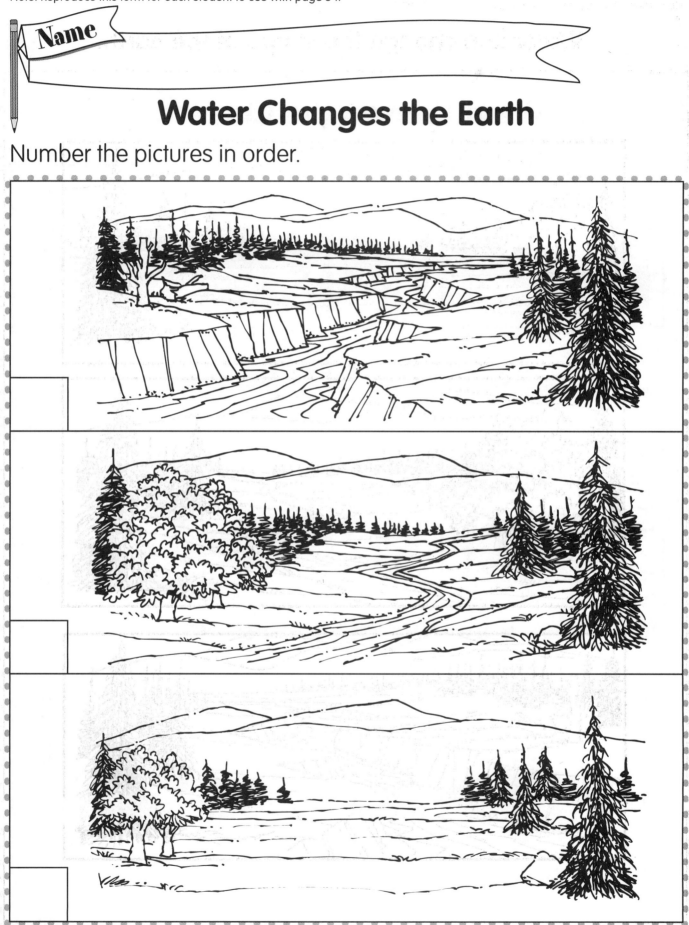

Name

What Caused the Change?

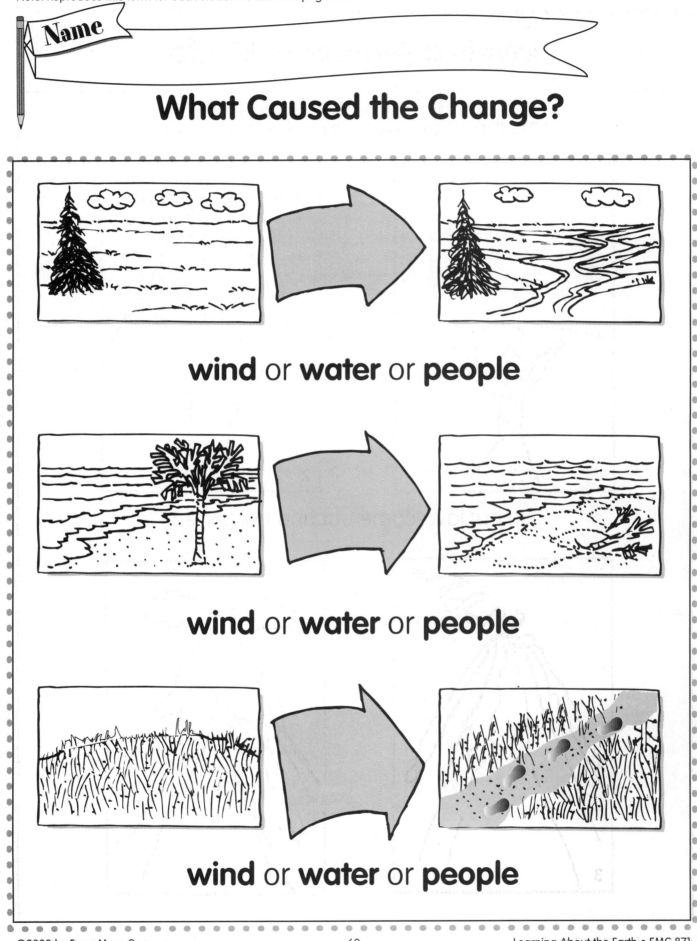

wind or **water** or **people**

wind or **water** or **people**

wind or **water** or **people**

How Is a Mountain Made?

This mountain was made by a volcano.

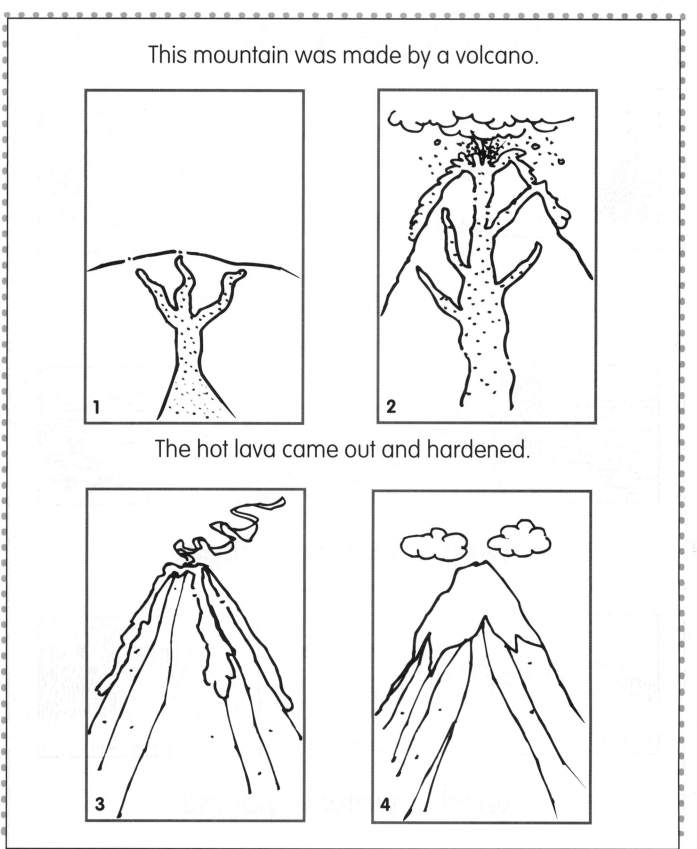

The hot lava came out and hardened.

How Is a Mountain Made?

This mountain was made by an earthquake.
The land was "pushed up."

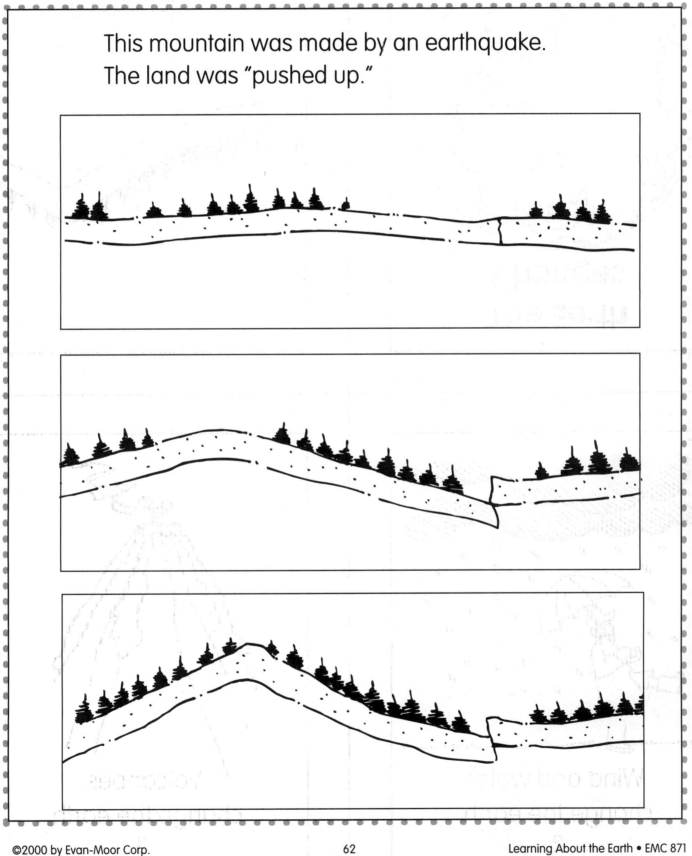

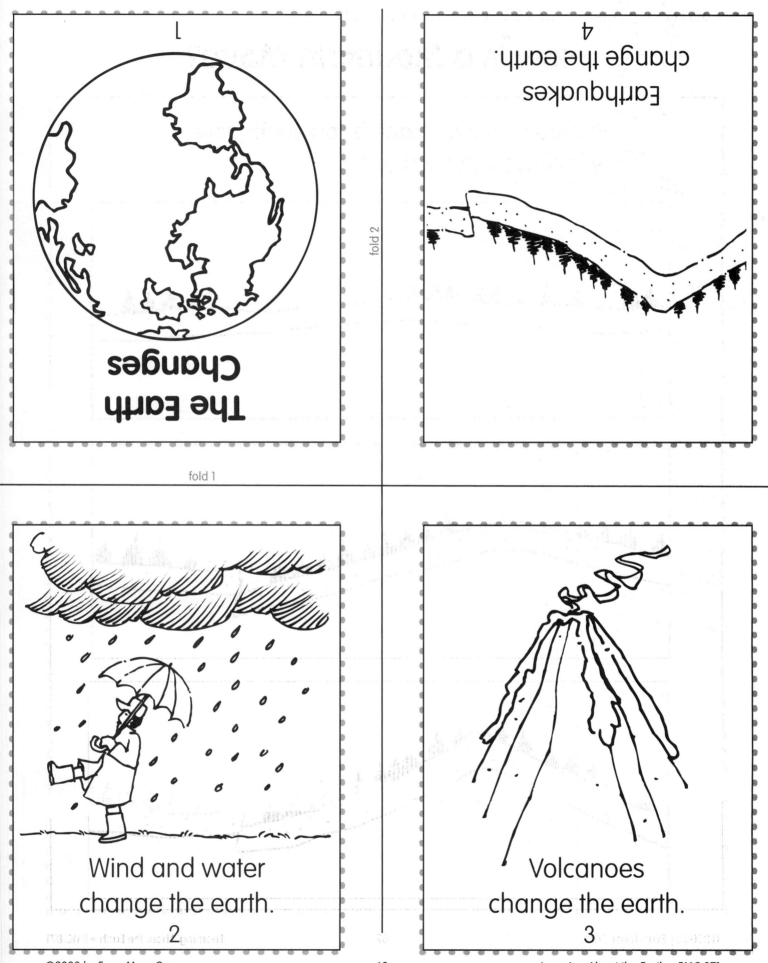

The Earth Changes

1

fold 2

Earthquakes change the earth.

4

fold 1

Wind and water change the earth.

2

Volcanoes change the earth.

3

Learning About the Earth • EMC 871

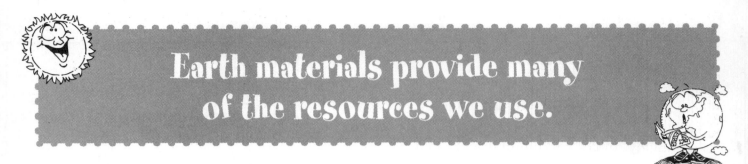
The Resources We Use Come from the Earth

- Engage students in a discussion of what they have used today. Ask, "What did you use when you ate lunch?" *(sandwich, apple, milk, lunch box, napkin)* "What did you use when you got dressed for school?" *(soap and water, toothbrush, comb, shoes)* "What did you use when you were at school?" *(book, paper, pencil, scissors)*

- List their responses on a sheet of chart paper.

Things We Use Come From the Earth

apple	paper
milk	scissors
soap	wood
water	pencil

- Read appropriate parts of *You're Aboard Spaceship Earth* by Patricia Lauber to discover some of the resources we get from the earth. Make additions and corrections to the chart started above.

- Have students complete page 67 by drawing three resources that come from the earth.

We Can Take Care of the Earth

- Ask students to think of ways that they can be more careful in using the earth's resources. Guide them with questions if they have difficulty coming up with ideas.

- Using page 68, students draw a line from each child to the correct answer.

pages 67 and 68

Keeping the Earth Clean

page 69

- Discuss how we affect the earth, using the transparency on page 69. Have students find all the ways people can help turn a dirty park into a clean one.

- Brainstorm to list all the ways your students can think of to keep their part of the world clean. Then have them clean up an area such as the playground or a neighborhood park.

- Give each student a large sheet of art paper. They are to fold the paper in half. On one half draw a picture of a messy/dirty area. On the other half draw the same place cleaned up.

- Read and discuss appropriate parts of *Common Ground: The Water, Earth, and Air We Share* by Molly Bang.

- Read and discuss *Celebrating Earth Day* by Janet McDonnell. Brainstorm to list ways they might celebrate the occasion.

- Set up a painting area with sheets of paper and tempera. Have students paint pictures of a clean Earth. Add the words "Keep Our Earth Clean" to the pictures. Hang these around the school as environmental posters.

Recycle to Save Resources

- Explain how important it is to cut down on the amount of garbage we create. Ask students to think of ways this can be done. List their responses on the chalkboard.

- Read and discuss the minibook on pages 70–72. Ask students to give examples of each way to save resources.

- Take a field trip to the local landfill so students can see where their garbage goes.

- Set up a class recycling center for supplies. (Have a place where colored art paper, old crayons, etc., can be sorted by color for children to use in other projects.)

use paper on both sides

save cans and bottles

don't waste food

pages 70–72

  Encourage students to be careful of how they use supplies (use both sides of a sheet of paper; don't throw away crayons because they are broken; sharpen pencils only when they really need it), and to use items from the recycling center whenever possible.

- Visit a recycling center.

- Create a list of ways they have learned to save resources.

- Make recycle bags to take home. Ask parents to send large brown grocery bags to class. Have students paint designs on the bags. Label the bags for the items to be recycled—cans, glass, newspapers. Send the bags home along with a letter to parents encouraging them to use the bags.

Logbook

Include these pages in each student's logbook.

 Learning About the Earth • EMC 871

Name

What Does the Earth Give Us?

Draw three things we use that come from the earth.

Name

Helping the Earth

Who is helping the earth?
Who is not helping?
Draw lines from each child to the correct answer.

Clean Up the Park

Taking Care of the Earth

Name:

1

How can we help take care of our earth?
We can fix things that are broken.

2

Learning About the Earth • EMC 871

We can give away things we don't need anymore.

3

Learning About the Earth • EMC 871

We can recycle cans, glass, and newspaper.

paper   glass   cans

4

We can use things up.

5

Draw a way you can take care of the earth.

6

Learning About the Earth • EMC 871

Fossils tell us about life long ago.

Plants and Animals Lived Long Ago

pages 75–77

- Read *Fossils Tell of Long Ago* by Aliki. Explain that this book tells us about animals and plants that lived a very long time ago. Ask students how we know this is true.

  Allow time for the students to share what they know about dinosaurs and fossils. Then show the pictures of fossils from pages 75–77. Ask questions such as, "Does this picture show the fossil of a plant or an animal? How can you tell it was a (plant/animal)? What part of the (plant/animal) can you see in the fossil picture?" Then display the plant and animal cards. Ask students to match the plant or animal to the picture of its fossil.

- Record student responses on a chart.

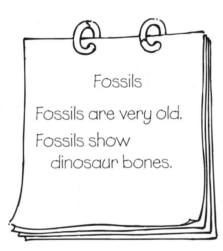

Fossils

Fossils are very old.

Fossils show
dinosaur bones.

page 78

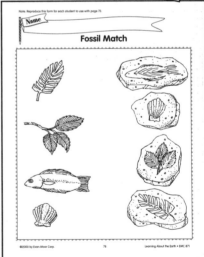

Fossil Match

- Using page 78, students match fossils to the correct animals and plants.

- Play "Fossil Concentration" using the cards on pages 75–77. The game can be played one of two ways—matching the same fossil (reproduce two sets of cards) or matching the fossil to the picture of its original plant or animal (reproduce one set of cards).

- Make fossil prints with your students, following the directions on page 74.

Fossil prints are fun to make.

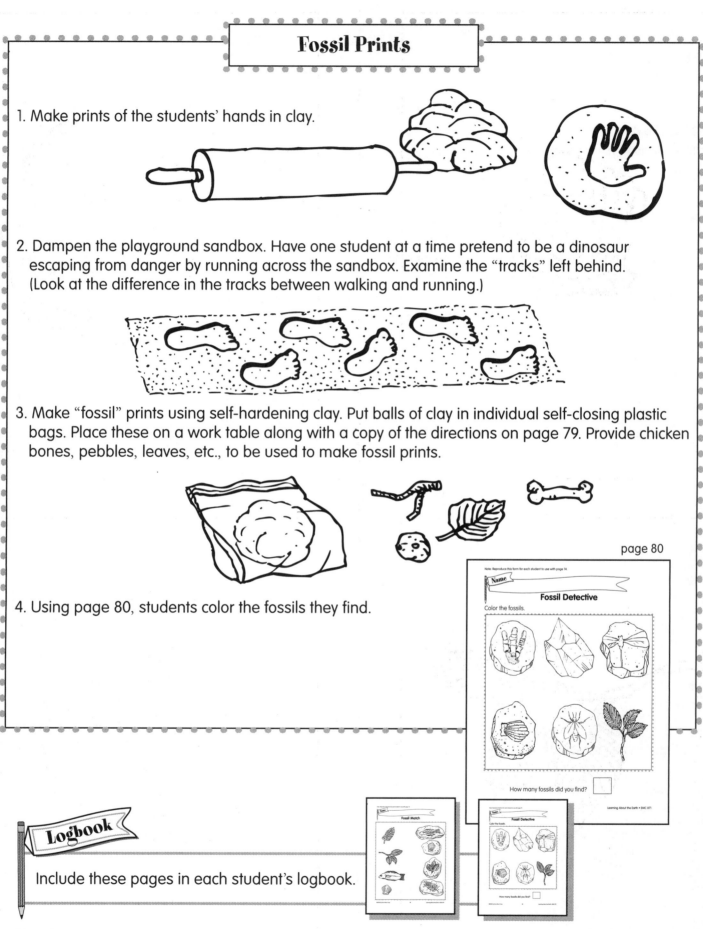

Fossil Prints

1. Make prints of the students' hands in clay.

2. Dampen the playground sandbox. Have one student at a time pretend to be a dinosaur escaping from danger by running across the sandbox. Examine the "tracks" left behind. (Look at the difference in the tracks between walking and running.)

3. Make "fossil" prints using self-hardening clay. Put balls of clay in individual self-closing plastic bags. Place these on a work table along with a copy of the directions on page 79. Provide chicken bones, pebbles, leaves, etc., to be used to make fossil prints.

page 80

4. Using page 80, students color the fossils they find.

Logbook

Include these pages in each student's logbook.

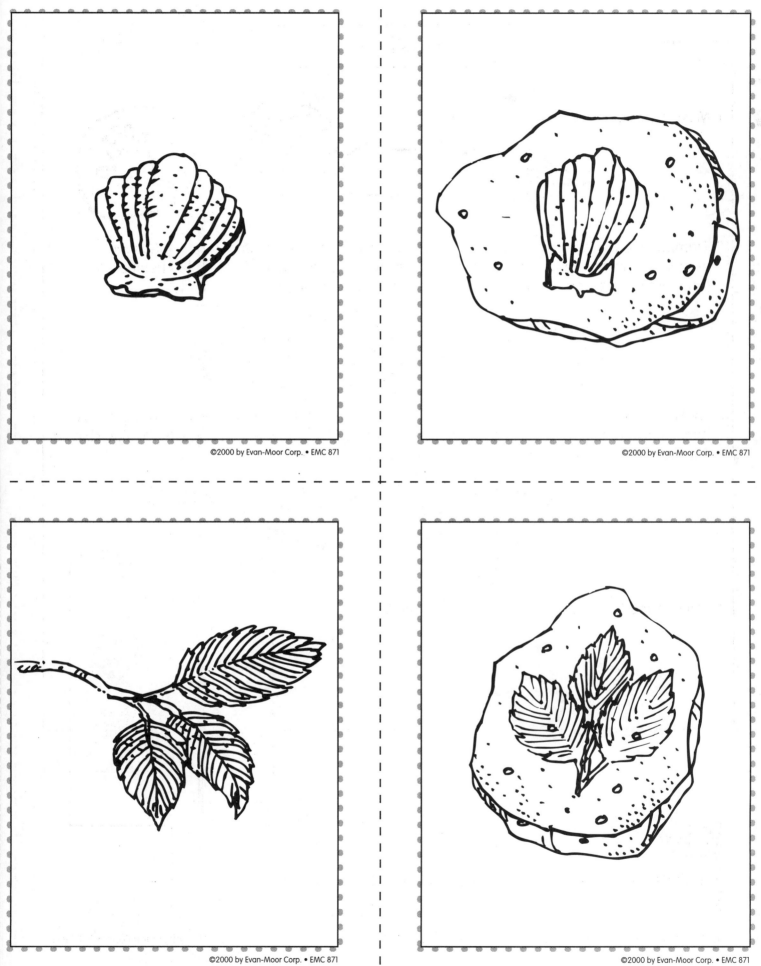

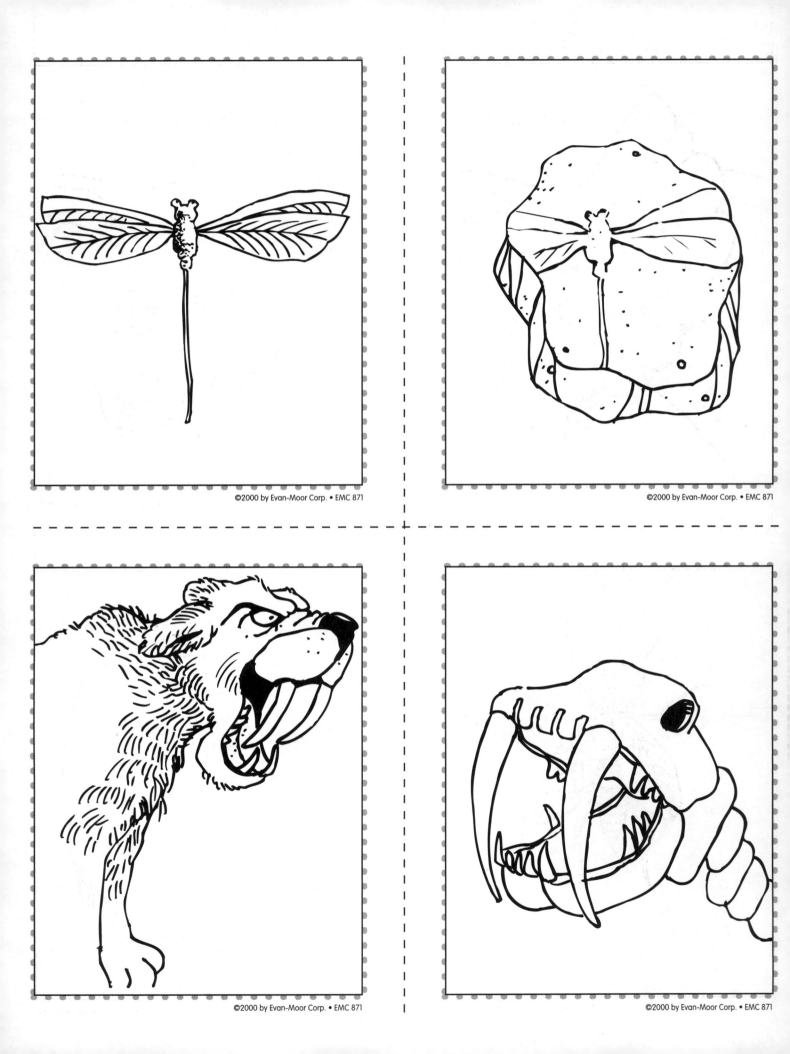

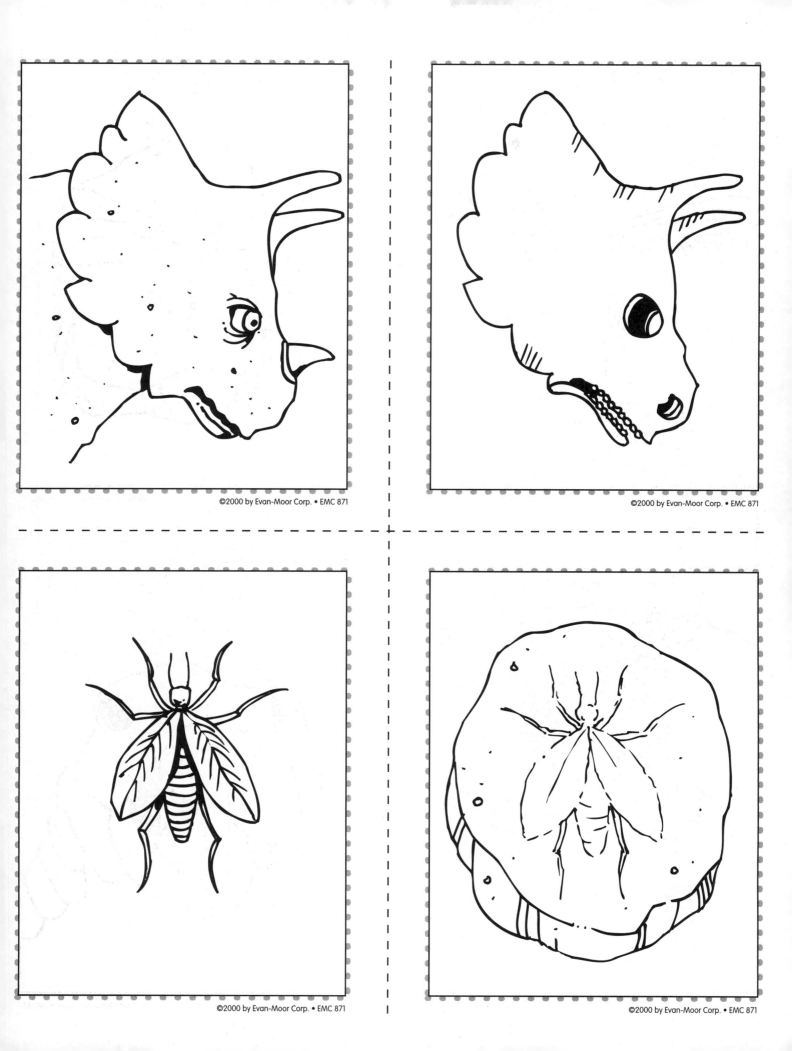

Name

Fossil Match

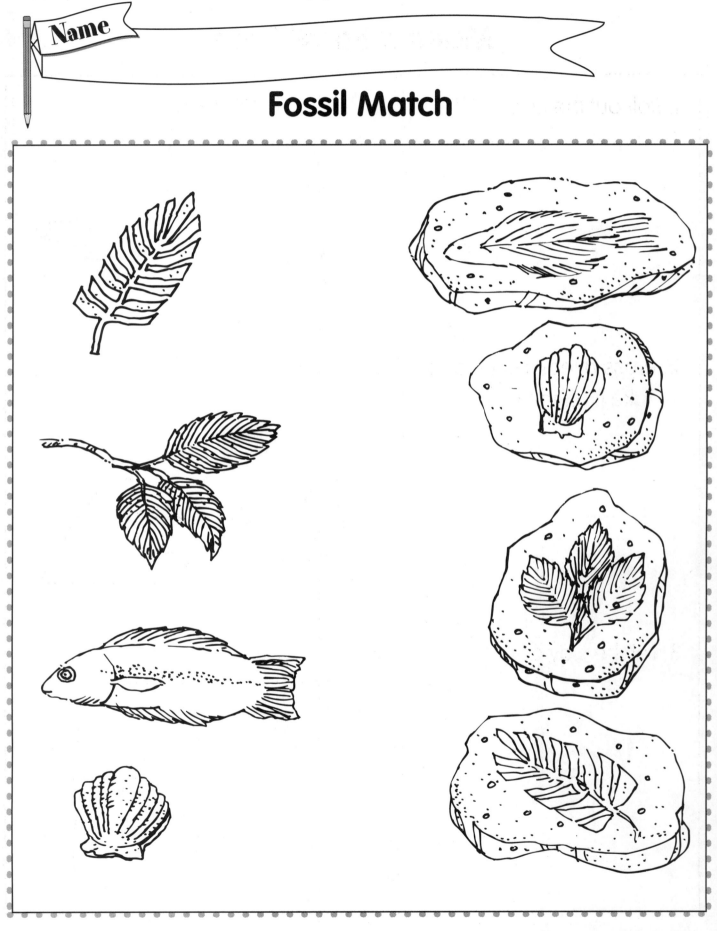

Make a Fossil Print

1. Roll out the clay.

2. Press a leaf, bone, or pebble into the clay.
   Take it off the clay.

3. Let the clay dry.

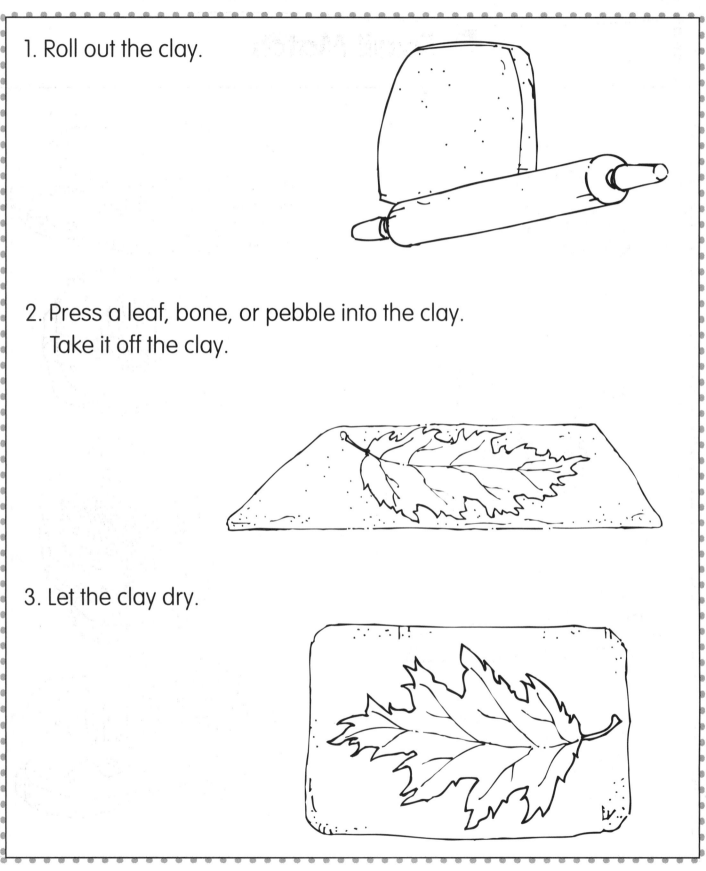

Name

Fossil Detective

Color the fossils.

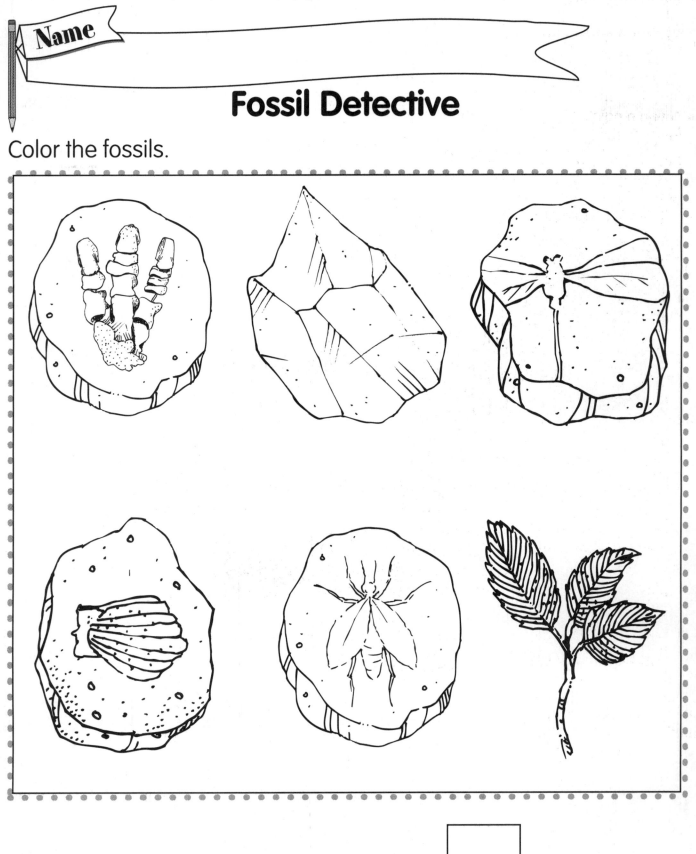

How many fossils did you find?